101 POEMS THAT COULD SAVE YOUR LIFE

101 POEMS
THAT COULD
SAVE YOUR LIFE

EDITED BY

DAISY GOODWIN

HarperCollins*Publishers*

HarperCollins*Publishers*
77–85 Fulham Palace Road,
Hammersmith, London W6 8JB

Published by HarperCollins*Publishers* 1999
18 17 16 15 14 13 12 11

Full permissions information may be found on pp. 139–142

A catalogue record for this book is
available from the British Library

ISBN 0 00 257072 6

Set in Postscript Linotype Minion by
Rowland Phototypesetting Ltd,
Bury St Edmunds, Suffolk

Printed and bound in Great Britain by
The Bath Press Ltd, Bath

For my mother

CONTENTS

INTRODUCTION ix

Apologies 3
Bad hair day 5
Bereavement 7
Big decision 10
Birthday blues 13
Career crisis 15
Christmas 19
Commitment problems 22
Divorce 28
Don't let the bastards get you
  down 33
Famous for fifteen minutes 39
First date 41
First wrinkle 44
Football widow 46
Friendship 47
Getting married 50
Hangovers 52
Illness 53
Insomnia 56
Instant moral fibre (modern
  mantras) 57
Is this relationship going
  anywhere? 65
Is this the real thing? 70
Just do it 75

Monday morning 79
Money worries 80
Morning after 82
Mothers-in-law 86
Moving house 88
New baby 92
New year's resolutions 97
Parenthood 99
Playing away 102
Retail therapy 108
Rock bottom 109
S.A.D. 113
School 115
Staying married 116
Stressed out 119
Successfully single 124
When you lose your pet 130
When your lover has gone 132

ACKNOWLEDGEMENTS 139
EMOTIONAL INDEX 143

INTRODUCTION

Problems can make you lonely. They hurtle around your head refusing to be pinned down. Problems are possessive, they belong to you and nobody else, no way. Most over the counter solutions to life's ills come with problems of their own: Prozac shrivels your sex life, Viagra gives you headaches, drink ruins your looks, therapy is expensive and self-help books are by and large unreadable, printed on the sort of paper that leaves ink on your hands, and impossible to read in public. It's bad enough being a woman who loves too much without all the other passengers on the Central Line knowing as well. There are friends, of course, but how many of them can listen to your problems without a grain of smugness? But there is an alternative: for quick and effective relief for all your emotional ailments without harmful side effects, try a poem – for however bad it is, however low you have sunk you can be sure that some poet has been there too.

The right poem at the right time, the right words in the right order can put all those whirling thoughts to rest. It can show you a way through or it can give you a shield to hide behind. It can turn the light back on in a place you thought was permanently disconnected. It can be a talisman to be worn in the head, proof against modern miseries. It can lie for years dusty with neglect until one day its meaning becomes clear, recognition blows away the cobwebs. The right poem at the right time can change your life.

I decided to put this book together because that happened to me. Once I was struggling with one of those decisions that seemed terrifying whichever way I looked at it. Should I jump or turn back the way I had come? Finally a wise friend, exasperated with my endlessly circular arguments, found me a poem, 'The Big Decision' by Cavafy. She shoved it in my hand and walked off. It goes:

> For some people the day comes
> when they have to declare the great Yes
> or the great No. It's clear at once who has the Yes
> ready within him: and saying it
>
> he goes from honour to honour, strong in his conviction.
> He who refuses does not repent. Asked again,
> he'd still say no. Yet that no – the right no –
> drags him down all his life.

As I read it I felt all the barriers in my head falling away. Afterwards it seemed such an easy choice, but it wasn't until I collided with that poem that I found the energy to go ahead. There have been plenty of other occasions where the right poem has taken the edge off a pain, sanded down a disappointment, put a percentage point on happiness. There may not be a cure but there is always a consolation.

To use this book for self-help purposes, first turn to the emotional index to find the condition from which you are currently suffering. If you don't know exactly what the problem is, but the future seems hopeless, then I suggest you go straight to the 'Instant Moral Fibre' section. Just the process of reading them is a step towards clarifying your own thoughts. These are the rugged poems with lots of handholds to pull you out of your misery. If you feel that everyone is out to get you then turn straight to the 'Don't Let the Bastards Get You Down' pages which might give you some ammunition, or maybe just the strength to turn away. If your problems are love related then there are entries for every swoop of the emotional rollercoaster from 'First Date' to 'Is This Relationship Going Anywhere?' and 'When Your Lover Has Gone'. And if you've just said good-bye to love, there is a whole section on being 'Successfully Single'. There are poems here to console you as you pass the bleaker milestones: discovering the first wrinkle, those accumulating birthdays, the death of someone close, and poems to make you smile through lighter skirmishes with misfortune: bad hair days, insomnia, Monday mornings, babies that won't stop crying, Christmas.

As with any powerful remedy, anyone reading this book should read the instructions carefully. Chronic procrastinators should NOT put off turning to the 'Just Do It' entry, but these poems will only make things worse for the 'Stressed Out' who have their own section (which in turn the procrastinators should avoid at all costs). Of course you could just read the book straight through, but you can hear the right poem much more clearly if it's not muffled by layers of other voices. Using the index might help you make that direct connection which could just save your life. Poems are potent things, they should be taken in small doses.

Many of the poems in this book have found their place through personal recommendation: I have had suggestions from harassed working mothers, prisoners serving life for murder, happily married couples and chronic philanderers. Some poems are here because they worked for me, some just because they are good. Some poems are well-known, others are published here for the first time. I have tried, where possible, to include less well-known poems so that the reader has a good chance of encountering a poem that is completely new to them, with no classroom memories to dilute its strength.

After having the idea for this book I did nothing about it for months and then another friend showed me 'The Slow Starter' by Louis MacNeice, which contains the lines:

> Do not press me so, she said;
> Leave me alone and I will write
> But not just yet, I am sure you know
> The problem.

Reading it was enough to make me sit down at my desk immediately, in fact I taped it to the side of my computer with the last two lines highlighted in red pen, 'He turned and saw the accusing clock/ Race like a torrent round a rock.' It may not be MacNeice's greatest poem but it works.

I hope this will be a book to keep handy, next door to the medical encyclopedia, the telephone directories and the road maps. There are poems here for weddings, funerals, weeping friends, children leaving home, significant birthdays. On all those occasions when you don't know what to say, turn to this book and you may find that someone in this book has said it for you.

Finally a huge thankyou to all the people who suggested poems for this book: Joanna Coles, Peter Godwin, Nellie Hadzianesti, Ned Williams, Chloe Thomas and especially Wendy Cope. Special thanks to my sister Tabitha Potts for helping me put it together and Mary Enright and all the staff at the Poetry Library, the South Bank Centre, London, for their help and patience.

101 POEMS
THAT COULD
SAVE YOUR LIFE

APOLOGIES

Saying that you're sorry is one of the hardest things to pull off. If you sound too sorry then the recipient begins to think they may not have been angry enough in the first place, but if you don't sound sorry enough then it's worse than not apologizing at all. The Glyn Maxwell poem is charmingly sorry. If you felt bad enough to flagrantly disregard the rules of copyright you could fax it to the injured party and it might make them smile long enough to forgive you. I can't vouch for whether it works with bank managers though.

Deep Sorriness Atonement Song

for missed appointment, BBC North, Manchester

The man who sold Manhattan for a halfway decent bangle,
He had talks with Adolf Hitler and could see it from his angle,
And he heard the Silver Beatles but he didn't think they'd make
  it
So he bought a cake on Pudding Lane and thought 'Oh well I'll
  bake it'.
      But his chances they were slim,
      And his brothers they were Grimm,
      And he's sorry, very sorry,
      But I'm sorrier than him.

And the drunken plastic surgeon who said 'I know, let's enlarge
  'em!'
And the bloke who told the Light Brigade 'Oh what the hell, let's
  charge 'em,'
The magician with an early evening gig on the *Titanic*,
And the Mayor who told the people of Atlantis not to panic,
      And the Dong about his nose,

3

And the Pobble *re* his toes,
They're all sorry, very sorry,
But I'm sorrier than those.

And don't forget the Bible, with the Sodomites and Judas,
And Onan who discovered something nothing was as rude as,
And anyone who reckoned it was City's year for Wembley,
And the kid who called Napoleon a shortarse in assembly,
    And the man who always smiles
    'Cause he knows I have his files,
    They're all sorry, truly sorry,
    But I'm sorrier by miles.

And Robert Falcon Scott who lost the race to a Norwegian,
And anyone who's ever spilt the pint of a Glaswegian,
Or told a Finn a joke or spent an hour with a Swiss-German,
Or got a mermaid in the sack and found it was a merman,
    Or him who smelt a rat,
    And got curious as a cat,
    They're all sorry, deeply sorry,
    But I'm sorrier than that.

All the people who were rubbish when we needed them to do it,
Whose wires crossed, whose spirit failed, who ballsed it up or
    blew it,
All notchers of *nul points* and all who have a problem Houston,
At least they weren't in Kensington when they should have been
    at Euston.
    For I didn't build the Wall
    And I didn't cause the Fall
    But I'm sorry, Lord I'm sorry,
    I'm the sorriest of all.

Glyn Maxwell

BAD HAIR DAY

These are poems for those days when you catch sight of some sad shambling creature in a shop window and realize with a hot gasp of horror that you are sneering at your own reflection; or for days when you go swimsuit shopping or when you wake up to find a pimple squatting firmly on the end of your nose.

Still To Be Neat

Still to be neat, still to be drest,
As you were going to a feast;
Still to be powder'd, still perfum'd:
Lady, it is to be presum'd,
Though art's hid causes are not found,
All is not sweet, all is not sound.

Give me a look, give me a face
That makes simplicity a grace;
Robes loosely flowing, hair as free:
Such sweet neglect more taketh me
Than all th'adulteries of art;
They strike mine eyes, but not my heart.

Ben Jonson

The Fat Lady's Request

I, too, will disappear, will
Escape into centuries of darkness.

Come here and give me a cuddle,
Sit on my lap and give me a hug

While we are both still enjoying
This mysterious whirling planet.

And if you find me fat, you find me
Also, easy to find, very easy to find.

Joyce la Verne

BEREAVEMENT

In times of great pain some poems can organize grief and give it a shape that you can recognize and make room for. When I was producing the *Bookworm* programme for BBC1, the parents of a soldier killed in action in Northern Ireland read a poem which he had sent to them to be opened in the event of his death. It begins, 'Do not stand at my grave and weep'. No one knows who wrote the poem; a Navajo chief or a Victorian lady poet have been suggested, but wherever it comes from it is clearly a charm against the awful reality of death, 'Do not stand at my grave and cry; I am not there. I did not die.' The Auden poem is for the next stage in the grieving process when shock and denial give way to rage and sorrow. There's no hope in this poem, but surely it gives desolation its limits. The Ted Hughes poem from *Birthday Letters* is for later, when an eggshell thin crust of indifference has formed over that first gaping hole and then you trip over something shiny from the past and the tears start again.

Do not Stand at my Grave and Weep

Do not stand at my grave and weep;
I am not there. I do not sleep.
I am a thousand winds that blow.
I am the diamond glints on snow.
I am the sunlight on ripened grain.
I am the gentle autumn rain.
When you awaken in the morning's hush
I am the swift uplifting rush
Of quiet birds in circled flight.
I am the soft stars that shine at night.
Do not stand at my grave and cry;
I am not there. I did not die.

Funeral Blues

Stop all the clocks, cut off the telephone,
Prevent the dog from barking with a juicy bone,
Silence the pianos and with muffled drum
Bring out the coffin, let the mourners come.

Let aeroplanes circle moaning overhead
Scribbling on the sky the message He Is Dead,
Put crepe bows round the white necks of the public doves,
Let the traffic policemen wear black cotton gloves.

He was my North, my South, my East and West,
My working week and my Sunday rest,
My noon, my midnight, my talk, my song;
I thought that love would last for ever: I was wrong.

The stars are not wanted now: put out every one;
Pack up the moon and dismantle the sun;
Pour away the ocean and sweep up the wood;
For nothing now can ever come to any good.

W. H. Auden

A Short Film

It was not meant to hurt.
It had been made for happy remembering
By people who were still too young
To have learned about memory.

Now it is a dangerous weapon, a time-bomb,
Which is a kind of body-bomb, long-term, too.
Only film, a few frames of you skipping, a few seconds,
You aged about ten there, skipping and still skipping.

Not very clear grey, made out of mist and smudge,
This thing has a fine fuse, less a fuse
Than a wavelength attuned, an electronic detonator
To what lies in your grave inside us.

And how that explosion would hurt
Is not just an idea of horror but a flash of fine sweat
Over the skin-surface, a bracing of nerves
For something that has already happened.

Ted Hughes

BIG DECISION

Every important decision involves a loss of some kind, and sometimes the losses can seem much greater than the gains. I have often found myself in a position where I feel unable to move forward or back, trapped in the endless hypothetical arguments of indecision. The C. P. Cavafy poem snapped something for me when I read it. It was that phrase 'the right no'; I realized at this point that I would rather say 'yes' even if it was the wrong 'yes'. Robert Frost makes the point that every decision involves the giving up of a certain kind of future – the question is whether you tell of this loss with a sigh or whether you just let it go. The Wendy Cope poem is for those times when, as Lorelei Lee would say, 'fate just keeps on happening'.

Bloody Men

Bloody men are like bloody buses –
You wait for about a year
And as soon as one approaches your stop
Two or three others appear.

You look at them flashing their indicators,
Offering you a ride.
You're trying to read the destinations,
You haven't much time to decide.

If you make a mistake, there is no turning back.
Jump off, and you'll stand there and gaze
While the cars and the taxis and lorries go by
And the minutes, the hours, the days.

Wendy Cope

Che Fece . . . Il Gran Rifiuto

For some people the day comes
when they have to declare the great Yes
or the great No. It's clear at once who has the Yes
ready within him; and saying it,

he goes from honour to honour, strong in his conviction.
He who refuses does not repent. Asked again,
he'd still say no. Yet that no – the right no –
drags him down all his life.

C. P. Cavafy

The Road Not Taken

Two roads diverged in a yellow wood,
And sorry I could not travel both
And be one traveler, long I stood
And looked down one as far as I could
To where it bent in the undergrowth;

Then took the other, as just as fair,
And having perhaps the better claim,
Because it was grassy and wanted wear;
Though as for that, the passing there
Had worn them really about the same.

And both that morning equally lay
In leaves no step had trodden black.
Oh, I kept the first for another day!
Yet knowing how way leads on to way,
I doubted if I should ever come back.

I shall be telling this with a sigh
Somewhere ages and ages hence:
Two roads diverged in a wood, and I –
I took the one less traveled by,
And that has made all the difference.

Robert Frost

BIRTHDAY BLUES

After thirty every birthday feels a little bluer and I'm afraid these poems can be no more than consolations. But Swift's poem to Stella made this thirtysomething laugh, and the Frost poem is a useful vaccine against fiftysomething pomposity. If these poems are not enough, I suggest you look in the 'First Wrinkle' section.

Stella's Birthday

Stella this day is thirty-four,
(We shan't dispute a year or more:)
However Stella, be not troubled,
Although thy size and years are doubled,
Since first I saw thee at sixteen,
The brightest virgin on the green.
So little is thy form declined;
Made up so largely in thy mind.

Oh, would it please the gods to *split*
Thy beauty, size, and years, and wit,
No age could furnish out a pair
Of nymphs so graceful, wise and fair:
With half the lustre of your eyes,
With half your wit, your years, and size:
And then before it grew too late,
How should I beg of gentle fate,
(That either nymph might have her swain,)
To split my worship too in twain.

Jonathan Swift

What Fifty Said

When I was young my teachers were the old.
I gave up fire for form till I was cold.
I suffered like a metal being cast.
I went to school to age to learn the past.

Now I am old my teachers are the young.
What can't be molded must be cracked and sprung.
I strain at lessons fit to start a suture.
I go to school to youth to learn the future.

Robert Frost

CAREER CRISIS

It's easy to find lifesaving love poems, but useful work poems are in short supply. Lots of poets have had perfectly regular jobs, T. S. Eliot worked in a bank, Wallace Stevens was something in insurance, but neither wanted to write about it. Philip Larkin was the librarian of Hull University, and by all accounts a very good one, but he was seriously ambivalent about the whole business, 'Why should I let the toad *work* squat on my life?' It's a question we've all asked ourselves. But before you hand in a letter of resignation read to the end of the poem. I first read the Julie O'Callaghan poem when I was conducting 'performance appraisals' at the BBC, a process which was bringing out my latent sadism. I hope this poem made the experience a little more bearable for my appraisees. (And if it didn't then I refer any of them that happen to be reading this to the Apology section.) I think this poem is required reading for anyone who's been sent on a management training course.

Managing the Common Herd:

two approaches for senior management

THEORY X: People are naturally lazy.
They come late, leave early, feign illness.
When they sit at their desks
it's ten to one they're yakking to colleagues
on the subject of who qualifies as a gorgeous hunk.
They're coating their lips and nails with slop,
a magazine open to 'What your nails say about you'
or 'Ten exercises to keep your bottom in top form'
under this year's annual report.
These people need punishment;
they require stern warnings
and threats – don't be a coward,

don't be intimidated by a batting eyelash.
Stand firm: a few tears, a Mars Bar,
several glasses of cider with her pals tonight
and you'll be just the same old
rat-bag, mealy-mouthed, small-minded tyrant
you were before you docked her
fifteen minutes pay for insubordination.

Never let these con-artists get the better of you.

THEORY Z: Staff need encouragement.
Give them a little responsibility
and watch their eager faces lighting up.
Let them know their input is important.
Be democratic – allow all of them
their two cents worth of gripes.
(Don't forget this is the Dr Spock generation.)
If eight out of twelve of them
prefer green garbage cans to black ones
under their desks, be generous –
the dividends in productivity
will be reaped with compound interest.
Offer incentives, show them
it's to their *own* advantage to meet targets.
Don't talk down to your employees.
Make staff believe that they
have valid and innovative ideas
and that not only are you interested.
but that you will act upon them.

Remember, they're human too.

Julie O'Callaghan

Toads

Why should I let the toad *work*
   Squat on my life?
Can't I use my wit as a pitchfork
   And drive the brute off?

Six days of the week it soils
   With its sickening poison –
Just for paying a few bills!
   That's out of proportion.

Lots of folk live on their wits:
   Lecturers, lispers,
Losels, loblolly-men, louts –
   They don't end as paupers;

Lots of folk live up lanes
   With fires in a bucket,
Eat windfalls and tinned sardines –
   They seem to like it.

Their nippers have got bare feet,
   Their unspeakable wives
Are skinny as whippets – and yet
   No one actually *starves*.

Ah, were I courageous enough
  To shout *Stuff your pension!*
But I know, all too well, that's the stuff
  That dreams are made on:

For something sufficiently toad-like
  Squats in me, too;
Its hunkers are heavy as hard luck,
  And cold as snow,

And will never allow me to blarney
  My way to getting
The fame and the girl and the money
  All at one sitting.

I don't say, one bodies the other
  One's spiritual truth;
But I do say it's hard to lose either,
  When you have both.

Philip Larkin

CHRISTMAS

Christmas comes pretty high on the stressful event index, just after divorce and moving house. A recent experiment monitored the stress levels of a man going Christmas shopping in a department store and found them equal to those of a fighter pilot going into combat. The poems in this section are to reassure you that other people are suffering too. I particularly like the poem, 'Monstrous Ingratitude'. How often has a relationship faltered because of a carelessly thought through present?

Family Court

One would be in less danger
From the wiles of the stranger
If one's own kin and kith
Were more fun to be with.

Ogden Nash

God's Christmas Jokes

Christmas: there was the usual crop of disasters:
Planes, coaches, crashed.
(So often the victims are pilgrims
Or those on errands of mercy).

In the home, the disasters are on a less heroic scale,
The stressful, claustrophobic press
Of one's nearest and dearest
Being by far the worst.

The snappy rejoinders, early on suppressed,
And by Day Three not suppressed.
The bathroom used for a quick fit of sobbing
And phone calls late at night
From suicidal single friends
Who have missed out on Perfect Love at Christmas.

On the first day after Bank Holiday the Sales begin,
And people shoot out from their doors like prisoners released,
Glad to be finished with their attempts at Peace on Earth
And bursting with meaty energy for the fray.

Connie Bensley

Monstrous Ingratitude

Gifts as gulfs . . .
Thought prompted by one
from ice ages ago:
a lime-green cardigan,
a garment I've never worn
and never will wear.
I hid it in a drawer
and mainly it stays there,
except when, as today,
on the trail of a lost sock,
I dig it up and feel once more
that sundering shock.

With kept creases
and buttons still done,
it invariably releases
the same terror as when,
tearing the posh paper,
I saw at a glance
how little she understood me.
Well, I covered my inner silence
with mumbled thanks;
yet the rift persists
and even now
pride prevents me
from trying the thing on, somehow.

Boris Parkin

COMMITMENT PROBLEMS

This is the place to look if you are in love with a slippery person, or perhaps you're a slippery person yourself. We all know drifters like the man in Tony Hoagland's poem, 'It's the kind of perceptual confusion/ that makes your loved ones into strangers/ that makes a highway look like a woman/ with air conditioned arms'. Yeats yearns for that kind of freedom, 'the best thing is/ To change my loves while dancing/ And pay but a kiss for a kiss.' And Blake has the only way to deal with Peter Pans, male and female. It may not fulfil your inner needs but kissing 'the joy as it flies' means you might see them again. And the Alice Walker poem is a reminder that failure to commit can be a mutual thing.

I'm Really Very Fond

I'm really very fond of you,
he said.

I don't like fond.
It sounds like something
you would tell a dog.

Give me love,
or nothing.

Throw your fond in a pond,
I said.

But what I felt for him
was also warm, frisky,
moist-mouthed,
eager,
and could swim away

if forced to do so.

Alice Walker

The Collarbone of a Hare

Would I could cast a sail on the water
Where many a king has gone
And many a king's daughter,
And alight at the comely trees and the lawn,
The playing upon pipes and the dancing,
And learn that the best thing is
To change my loves while dancing
And pay but a kiss for a kiss.

I would find by the edge of that water
The collarbone of a hare
Worn thin by the lapping of water,
And pierce it through with a gimlet, and stare
At the old bitter world where they marry in churches,
And laugh over the untroubled water
At all who marry in churches,
Through the white thin bone of a hare.

W. B. Yeats

Eternity

He who binds to himself a joy
Does the winged life destroy;
But he who kisses the joy as it flies
Lives in eternity's sun rise.

William Blake

Perpetual Motion

In a little while I'll be drifting up on an on-ramp,
sipping coffee from a styrofoam container,
checking my gas gauge with one eye
and twisting the dial of the radio
with the fingers of my third hand,
looking for a station I can steer to Saturn on.

It seems I have the traveling disease
again, an outbreak of that virus
celebrated by the cracked lips
of a thousand blues musicians — song
about a rooster and a traintrack,
a sunrise and a jug of cherry cherry wine.

It's the kind of perceptual confusion
that makes your loved ones into strangers,
that makes a highway look like a woman
with air conditioned arms. With a
bottomless cup of coffee for a mouth
and jewelry shaped like pay phone booths
dripping from her ears.

In a little while the radio will
almost have me convinced
that I am doing something romantic,
something to do with 'freedom' and 'becoming'
instead of fright and flight into
an anonymity so deep

it has no bottom,
only signs tell you what direction
you are falling in: CHEYENNE, SEATTLE,
WICHITA, DETROIT — Do you hear me,
do you feel me moving through?
With my foot upon the gas,
between the future and the past,
I am here —
here where the desire to vanish
is stronger than the desire to appear.

Tony Hoagland

DIVORCE

Read Vicky Feaver's poem first if you're contemplating divorce out of boredom. Her rather bleak message is that even those who swap one partner for another will end up 'Just like the rest of us'. But if you're a wife who's decided to go then read 'A Woman's Work'. And I like Sophie Hannah's poem very much: relationships should end with a bang not with a whimper. When it's all over and you are trying to find a way of dealing with it in your head, read 'Wedding-Ring' by Denise Levertov.

The Way We Live

In rooms whose lights
On winter evenings
Make peepshows of our lives –

Behind each window
A stage so cluttered up
With props and furniture

It's not surprising
We make a mess of what began
So simply with *I love you*.

Look at us: some
Slumped in chairs
And hardly ever speaking

And others mouthing
The same tired lines to ears
That long ago stopped listening.

Once we must have dreamed
Of something better.
But even those who swapped

One partner for another
Have ended up
Just like the rest of us:

Behind doors, moving outside
Only to go to work
Or spend weekends with mother.

Vicki Feaver

Wedding-Ring

My wedding-ring lies in a basket
as if at the bottom of a well.
Nothing will come to fish it back up
and onto my finger again.
                              It lies
among keys to abandoned houses,
nails waiting to be needed and hammered
into some wall,
telephone numbers with no names attached,
idle paperclips.
                    It can't be given away
for fear of bringing ill-luck.
                    It can't be sold
for the marriage was good in its own
time, though that time is gone.
                    Could some artificer
beat into it bright stones, transform it
into a dazzling circlet no one could take
for solemn betrothal or to make promises
living will not let them keep? Change it
into a simple gift I could give in friendship?

Denise Levertov

A Woman's Work

Will you forgive me that I did not run
to welcome you as you came in the door?
Forgive I did not sew your buttons on
and left a mess strewn on the kitchen floor?
A woman's work is never done
and there is more.

The things I did I should have left undone
the things I lost that I could not restore;
Will you forgive I wasn't any fun?
Will you forgive I couldn't give you more?
A woman's work is never done
and there is more.

I never finished what I had begun,
I could not keep the promises I swore,
so we fought battles neither of us won
and I said 'Sorry!' and you banged the door.
A woman's work is never done
and there is more.

But in the empty space now you are gone
I find the time I didn't have before.
I lock the house and walk out to the sun
where the sea beats upon a wider shore
and woman's work is never done,
not any more.

Dorothy Nimmo

The End of Love

The end of love should be a big event.
It should involve the hiring of a hall.
Why the hell not? It happens to us all.
Why should it pass without acknowledgement?

Suits should be dry-cleaned, invitations sent.
Whatever form it takes – a tiff, a brawl –
The end of love should be a big event.
It should involve the hiring of a hall.

Better than the unquestioning descent
Into the trap of silence, than the crawl
From visible to hidden, door to wall.

Get the announcement made, the money spent.
The end of love should be a big event.
It should involve the hiring of a hall.

Sophie Hannah

DON'T LET THE BASTARDS GET YOU DOWN

Read these poems before you have the second martini, or leave an abusive message on an innocent answering-machine. In the right mood reading these poems will give you the same rush as playing 'I Will Survive' at full volume. Lots of women have recommended the Maya Angelou poem; one of them described it as 'instant invincibility'. And for men who feel uneasy about all that talk of 'oil wells in her walk' there is W. E. Henley's 'Invictus', 'I am the master of my fate: I am the captain of my soul'. Just saying it makes the sinews stiffen. Perfect if you've just been sacked.

If People Disapprove of You

Make being disapproved of your hobby.
Make being disapproved of your aim.
Devise new ways of scoring points
In the Being Disapproved Of Game.

Let them disapprove in their dozens.
Let them disapprove in their hordes.
You'll find that being disapproved of
Builds character, brings rewards

Just like any form of striving.
Don't be arrogant; don't coast
On your high disapproval rating.
Try to be disapproved of most.

At this point, if it's useful,
Draw a pie-chart or a graph.
Show it to someone who disapproves.
When they disapprove, just laugh.

Count the emotions you provoke:
Anger, suspicion, shock.
One point for each of these and two
For every boat you rock.

Feel yourself warming to your task –
You do it bloody well.
At last you've found an area
In which you can excel.

Savour the thrill of risk without
The fear of getting caught.
Whether they sulk or scream or pout,
Enjoy your new-found sport.

Meanwhile all those who disapprove
While you are having fun
Won't even know your game exists
So tell yourself you've won.

Sophie Hannah

To A Friend Whose Work Has Come to Nothing

Now all the truth is out,
Be secret and take defeat
From any brazen throat,
For how can you compete,
Being honour bred, with one
Who, were it proved he lies,
Were neither shamed in his own
Nor in his neighbours' eyes?
Bred to a harder thing
Than Triumph, turn away
And like a laughing string
Whereon mad fingers play
Amid a place of stone,
Be secret and exult,
Because of all things known
That is most difficult.

W. B. Yeats

Invictus

Out of the night that covers me,
  Black as the pit from pole to pole,
I thank whatever gods may be
  For my unconquerable soul.

In the fell clutch of circumstance
  I have not winced nor cried aloud:
Under the bludgeonings of chance
  My head is bloody, but unbowed.

Beyond this place of wrath and tears
  Looms but the Horror of the shade,
And yet the menace of the years
  Finds and shall find me unafraid.

It matters not how strait the gate,
  How charged with punishments the scroll,
I am the master of my fate:
  I am the captain of my soul.

W. E. Henley

Still I Rise

You may write me down in history
With your bitter, twisted lies,
You may trod me in the very dirt
But still, like dust, I'll rise.

Does my sassiness upset you?
Why are you beset with gloom?
'Cause I walk like I've got oil wells
Pumping in my living room.

Just like moons and like suns,
With the certainty of tides,
Just like hopes springing high,
Still I'll rise.

Did you want to see me broken?
Bowed head and lowered eyes?
Shoulders falling down like teardrops,
Weakened by my soulful cries.

Does my haughtiness offend you?
Don't you take it awful hard
'Cause I laugh like I've got gold mines
Diggin' in my own back yard.

You may shoot me with your words,
You may cut me with your eyes,
You may kill me with your hatefulness,
But still, like air, I'll rise.

Does my sexiness upset you?
Does it come as a surprise
That I dance like I've got diamonds
At the meeting of my thighs?

Out of the huts of history's shame
I rise
Up from a past that's rooted in pain
I rise
I'm a black ocean, leaping and wide,
Welling and swelling I bear in the tide.

Leaving behind nights of terror and fear
I rise
Into a daybreak that's wondrously clear
I rise
Bringing the gifts that my ancestors gave,
I am the dream and the hope of the slave.
I rise
I rise
I rise.

Maya Angelou

FAMOUS FOR FIFTEEN MINUTES

You might not need this, but then you might win the lottery . . . or fall in love with a member of the royal family.

How to Deal with the Press

She'll urge you to confide. Resist.
Be careful, courteous, and cool.
Never trust a journalist.

'We're off the record,' she'll insist.
If you believe her, you're a fool.
She'll urge you to confide. Resist.

Should you tell her who you've kissed,
You'll see it all in print, and you'll
Never trust a journalist

Again. The words are hers to twist,
And yours the risk of ridicule.
She'll urge you to confide. Resist.

'But X is nice,' the publicist
Will tell you. 'We were friends at school.'
Never trust a journalist,

Hostile, friendly, sober, pissed,
Male or female – that's the rule.
When tempted to confide, resist.
Never trust a journalist.

Wendy Cope

FIRST DATE

Perhaps these two poems are a bit sober to be in a first date section, but you could always tuck them away with your other prophylactics.

Proposal

Let's fall in love —
In our mid-thirties
It's not only
Where the hurt is.

I won't get smashed up
Should you go
Away for weekends —
We both know

No two people
Can be completely
All-sufficient.
But twice weekly

We'll dine together
Split the bill,
Admire each other's
Wit. We will

Be splendid lovers,
Slow, well-trained,
Tactful, gracefully
Unrestrained.

You'll keep your flat
And I'll keep mine —
Our bank accounts
Shall not entwine.

We'll make the whole thing
Hard and bright.
We'll call it love —
We may be right.

Tom Vaughan

Social Note

Lady, lady, should you meet
One whose ways are all discreet,
One who murmurs that his wife
Is the lodestar of his life,
One who keeps assuring you
That he never was untrue,
Never loved another one . . .
Lady, lady, better run!

Dorothy Parker

FIRST WRINKLE

Jenny Joseph's 'Warning' is officially the nation's favourite modern poem –
everybody needs a way to acknowledge the inevitable – and Fleur Adcock's poem
is a reminder that it's not all downhill.

Kissing

The young are walking on the riverbank,
arms around each other's waist and shoulders,
pretending to be looking at the waterlilies
and what might be a nest of some kind, over
there, which two who are clamped together
mouth to mouth have forgotten about.
The others, making courteous detours
around them, talk, stop talking, kiss.
They can see no one older than themselves.
It's their river. They've got all day.

Seeing's not everything. At this very
moment the middle-aged are kissing
in the backs of taxis, on the way
to airports and stations. Their mouths and tongues
are soft and powerful and as moist as ever.
Their hands are not inside each other's clothes
(because of the driver) but locked so tightly
together that it hurts: it may leave marks
on their not of course youthful skin, which they won't
notice. They too may have futures.

Fleur Adcock

Warning

When I am an old woman I shall wear purple
With a red hat which doesn't go, and doesn't suit me.
And I shall spend my pension on brandy and summer gloves
And satin sandals, and say we've no money for butter.
I shall sit down on the pavement when I'm tired
And gobble up samples in shops and press alarm bells
And run my stick along the public railings
And make up for the sobriety of my youth.
I shall go out in my slippers in the rain
And pick the flowers in other people's gardens
And learn to spit.

You can wear terrible shirts and grow more fat
And eat three pounds of sausages at a go
Or only bread and pickle for a week
And hoard pens and pencils and beermats and things in boxes.

But now we must have clothes that keep us dry
And pay our rent and not swear in the street
And set a good example for the children.
We must have friends to dinner and read the papers.

But maybe I ought to practise a little now?
So people who know me are not too shocked and surprised
When suddenly I am old, and start to wear purple.

Jenny Joseph

FOOTBALL WIDOW

I suppose now that women have discovered football this poem is out of date, but there will always be male activities whose appeal is incomprehensible to women.

The Perfect Match

There is nothing like the five minutes to go:
Your lads one up, your lads one down, or the whole
 Thing even. How you actually feel,
  What you truly know,
Is that your lads are going to do it. So,

However many times in the past the fact
Is that they didn't, however you screamed and strained,
 Pummelled the floor, looked up and groaned
  As the Seiko ticked
On, when the ultimate ball is nodded or kicked.

The man in the air is you. Your beautiful wife
May curl in the corner yawningly calm and true,
 But something's going on with you
  That lasts male life.
Love's one thing, but this is the Big Chief.

Glyn Maxwell

FRIENDSHIP

Complicated webs of friendship have come to resemble and sometimes replace the extended families of the past. But while there are rules of engagement with families, the boundaries of friendship are less clearly defined. The Elizabeth Jennings poem is an affirmation of friendship, the Blake poem is a warning to grudge bearers, and the celebrated extract from one of John Donne's sermons is a reminder of why friendship is paramount.

I was angry with my friend;
I told my wrath, my wrath did end.
I was angry with my foe;
I told it not, my wrath did grow.

from 'A Poison Tree',
William Blake

No man is an island entire of itself; every man is a piece of the continent, a part of the main; if a clod be washed away by the sea, Europe is the less, as well as if a promontory were, as well as if a manor of thy friends' or of thine own were; any man's death diminishes me, because I am involved in mankind; and therefore never send to know for whom the bell tolls; it tolls for thee.

from *Devotions upon Emergent Occasions*
Meditation XVII
John Donne

Friendship

Such love I cannot analyse;
It does not rest in lips or eyes,
Neither in kisses nor caress.
Partly, I know, it's gentleness

And understanding in one word
Or in brief letters. It's preserved
By trust and by respect and awe.
These are the words I'm feeling for.

Two people, yes, two lasting friends.
The giving comes, the taking ends.
There is no measure for such things.
For this all Nature slows and sings.

Elizabeth Jennings

GETTING MARRIED

More and more people read poems at weddings, and the right one can be electrifying. I love this extract from 'The Prophet', it makes all the married people in the congregation shift a little in their seats: 'let there be spaces in your togetherness' is gilt-edged advice. The Edwin Muir poem is love the way it's meant to be, it's less well-known than 'The Prophet' and will put any mascara to the test.

Then Almitra spoke again and said, And what of Marriage, master?
And he answered saying:
Together you shall be for evermore.
But let there be spaces in your togetherness.
And let the winds of the heavens dance between you.

Love one another, but make not a bond of love.
Let it rather be a moving sea between the shores of your souls.
Fill each other's cup but drink not from one cup.
Give one another of your bread but eat not from the same loaf.
Sing and dance together and be joyous, but let each one of you be alone,
Even as the strings of a lute are alone though they quiver with the same music.

Give your hearts, but not into each other's keeping.
For only the hand of Life can contain your hearts.
And stand together yet not too near together:
For the pillars of the temple stand apart,
And the oak tree and the cypress grow not in each other's shadow.

from 'The Prophet',
Kahlil Gibran

The Confirmation

Yes, yours, my love, is the right human face.
I in my mind had waited for this long,
Seeing the false and searching for the true,
Then found you as a traveller finds a place
Of welcome suddenly amid the wrong
Valleys and rocks and twisting roads. But you,
What shall I call you? A fountain in a waste,
A well of water in a country dry,
Or anything that's honest and good, an eye
That makes the whole world bright. Your open heart,
Simple with giving, gives the primal deed,
The first good world, the blossom, the blowing seed,
The hearth, the steadfast land, the wandering sea.
Not beautiful or rare in every part.
But like yourself, as they were meant to be.

Edwin Muir

HANGOVERS

Byron clearly knew about hangovers, 'man being reasonable must get drunk; the best of life is but intoxication.' A white wine spritzer is much quicker than a twelve-step programme.

Hock and Soda Water

Few things surpass old wine; and they may preach
    Who please – the more because they preach in vain.
Let us have wine and woman, mirth and laughter,
Sermons and soda water the day after.

Man being reasonable must get drunk;
    The best of life is but intoxication.
Glory, the grape, love, gold, in these are sunk
    The hopes of all men and of every nation;
Without their sap, how branchless were the trunk
    Of life's strange tree, so fruitful on occasion.
But to return. Get very drunk, and when
You wake with headache, you shall see what then.

Ring for your valet, bid him quickly bring
    Some hock and soda water. Then you'll know
A pleasure worthy Xerxes, the great king;
    For not the blest sherbet, sublimed with snow,
Nor the first sparkle of the desert spring,
    Nor Burgundy in all its sunset glow,
After long travel, ennui, love, or slaughter,
Vie with that draught of hock and soda water.

from *Don Juan* Canto II
Lord Byron

ILLNESS

Both these poems have been recommended as lifesavers by people with serious illnesses. The Roger McGough poem was discovered by Steve, a fireman, at a time when he was undergoing treatment for a brain tumour and his wife was expecting twins. Steve found that the poem accurately described the way in which his illness had made him redefine his attitude to life. Something worked and Steve is now in remission. The Keats poem comes from a twenty-year-old student who is suffering from severe diabetes. The prognosis for her condition is only average but she finds this poem helps keep the despair at bay.

My Busconductor

My busconductor tells me
he only has one kidney
and that may soon go on strike
through overwork.
Each busticket
takes on now a different shape
and texture.
He holds a ninepenny single
as if it were a rose
and puts the shilling in his bag
as a child into a gasmeter.
His thin lips
have no quips
for fat factorygirls
and he ignores
the drunk who snores
and the oldman who talks to himself
and gets off at the wrong stop.

He goes gently to the bedroom
of the bus
to collect
and what familiar shops and pubs pass by
(perhaps for the last time ?).
The same old streets look different now
more distinct
as through new glasses.
And the sky
was it ever so blue?

And all the time
deepdown in the deserted busshelter of his mind
he thinks about his journey nearly done.
One day he'll clock on and never clock off
or clock off and never clock on.

Roger McGough

When I have Fears that I may Cease to be

When I have fears that I may cease to be
  Before my pen has gleaned my teeming brain,
Before high-piled books, in charactery,
  Hold like rich garners the full-ripened grain;
When I behold, upon the night's starred face,
  Huge cloudy symbols of a high romance,
And feel that I may never live to trace
  Their shadows, with the magic hand of chance;
And when I feel, fair creature of an hour!
  That I shall never look upon thee more,
Never have relish in the faery power
  Of reflecting love! – then on the shore
Of the wide world I stand alone, and think
  Till love and fame to nothingness do sink.

John Keats

INSOMNIA

I don't think this poem will actually help you sleep but it might cheer you up in the small hours.

Things

There are worse things than having behaved foolishly in public.
There are worse things than these miniature betrayals,
committed or endured or suspected; there are worse things
than not being able to sleep for thinking about them.
It is 5 a.m. All the worse things come stalking in
and stand icily about the bed looking worse and worse and
worse.

Fleur Adcock

INSTANT MORAL FIBRE (MODERN MANTRAS)

This is the place to look when you need a prescription for how to live on, a way to cope. The poems in this section are what I call 'modern mantras', the very act of reading them is somehow comforting, a way of moving from the heated present to a calmer place. Even if the poems' aspirations are staggering, you can't read a poem like Kipling's 'If' and not stand a little straighter. The Turkish poem by Hikmet that begins 'The best sea: has yet to be crossed' was written in prison and was recommended by another prisoner who said it gave him the strength to get to the end of his sentence. And make sure you read the Wendy Cope poem aloud, it's like doing a mental stretch class, you'll feel looser afterwards. The little Raymond Carver poem was written for his wife Tess Gallagher when he was dying of a brain tumour. I think it is a pretty good prescription for living.

If

If you can keep your head when all about you
   Are losing theirs and blaming it on you,
If you can trust yourself when all men doubt you,
   But make allowance for their doubting too;
If you can wait and not be tired by waiting,
   Or being lied about, don't deal in lies,
Or being hated, don't give way to hating,
   And yet don't look too good, nor talk too wise:

If you can dream – and not make dreams your master;
   If you can think – and not make thoughts your aim;
If you can meet with Triumph and Disaster
   And treat those two impostors just the same;
If you can bear to hear the truth you've spoken
   Twisted by knaves to make a trap for fools,

Or watch the things you gave your life to, broken,
And stoop and build 'em up with worn-out tools:

If you can make one heap of all your winnings
And risk it on one turn of pitch-and-toss,
And lose, and start again at your beginnings
And never breathe a word about your loss;
If you can force your heart and nerve and sinew
To serve your turn long after they are gone,
And so hold on when there is nothing in you
Except the Will which says to them: 'Hold on!'

If you can talk with crowds and keep your virtue,
Or walk with Kings – nor lose the common touch,
If neither foes nor loving friends can hurt you,
If all men count with you, but none too much;
If you can fill the unforgiving minute
With sixty seconds' worth of distance run,
Yours is the Earth and everything that's in it,
And – which is more – you'll be a Man, my son!

Rudyard Kipling

As Much as You Can

Even if you can't shape your life the way you want,
at least try as much as you can
not to degrade it
by too much contact with the world,
by too much activity and talk.

Do not degrade it by dragging it along,
taking it around and exposing it so often
to the daily silliness
of social relations and parties,
until it comes to seem a boring hanger-on.

C. P. Cavafy
translated from the Greek by Edmund Keeley and Philip Sherrard

24th September 1945

The best sea: has yet to be crossed.
The best child: has yet to be born.
The best days: have yet to be lived;
and the best word that I wanted to say to you
is the word that I have not yet said.

from 'Poems to Pirayé (his wife) from Prison'.
Nasim Hikmet
translated from the Turkish by Richard McKane

Leisure

What is this life if, full of care,
We have no time to stand and stare.

No time to stand beneath the boughs
And stare as long as sheep or cows.

No time to see, when woods we pass,
Where squirrels hide their nuts in grass.

No time to see, in broad daylight,
Streams full of stars, like skies at night.

No time to turn at Beauty's glance,
And watch her feet, how they can dance.

No time to wait till her mouth can
Enrich that smile her eyes began.

A poor life this if, full of care,
We have no time to stand and stare.

W. H. Davies

I Am Completely Different

I am completely different.
Though I am wearing the same tie as yesterday,
am as poor as yesterday,
as good for nothing as yesterday,
today
I am completely different.
Though I am wearing the same clothes,
am as drunk as yesterday,
living as clumsily as yesterday, nevertheless
today
I am completely different.

Ah –
I patiently close my eyes
on all the grins and smirks
on all the twisted smiles and horse laughs –
and glimpse then, inside me
one beautiful white butterfly
fluttering towards tomorrow.

Kuroda Saburo

The Ted Williams Villanelle

(for Ari Badaines)

'Don't let anybody mess with your swing.'
             Ted Williams, baseball player

Watch the ball and do your thing.
This is the moment. Here's your chance.
Don't let anybody mess with your swing.

It's time to shine. You're in the ring.
Step forward, adopt a winning stance,
Watch the ball and do your thing,

And while that ball is taking wing,
Run, without a backward glance.
Don't let anybody mess with your swing.

Don't let envious bastards bring
You down. Ignore the sneers, the can'ts.
Watch the ball and do your thing.

Sing out, if you want to sing.
Jump up, when you long to dance.
Don't let anybody mess with your swing.

Enjoy your talents. Have your fling.
The seasons change. The years advance.
Watch the ball and do your thing,
And don't let anybody mess with your swing.

Wendy Cope

Late Fragment

And did you get what
you wanted from this life, even so?
I did.
And what did you want?
To call myself beloved, to feel myself
beloved on the earth.

Raymond Carver
A New Path to the Waterfall

IS THIS RELATIONSHIP GOING ANYWHERE?

The modern dilemma. How good is good enough? Can relationships go up as well as down? Why do all other relationships look better than yours? The Meredith poem, 'Modern Love Sonnet 17' is worth remembering next time you go to a dinner party where everything seems irritatingly perfect, but your host and hostess could be playing 'hiding the skeleton'. 'Who's On First?', by the American poet Lloyd Schwartz, is a brilliant distillation of those circular conversations we've all had. And there might be some women who identify with 'Mrs Hobson's Choice'.

Modern Love, 17

At dinner, she is hostess, I am host.
Went the feast ever cheerfuller? She keeps
The Topic over intellectual deeps
In buoyancy afloat. They see no ghost.
With sparkling surface-eyes we ply the ball:
It is in truth a most contagious game:
HIDING THE SKELETON, shall be its name.
Such play as this, the devils might appal!
But here's the greater wonder; in that we
Enamoured of an acting nought can tire,
Each other, like true hypocrites, admire;
Warm-lighted looks, Love's ephemerioe,
Shoot gaily o'er the dishes and the wine.
We waken envy of our happy lot.
Fast, sweet, and golden, shows the marriage-knot.
Dear guests, you now have seen Love's corpse-light shine.

George Meredith

Mrs Hobson's Choice

What shall a woman
   Do with her ego,
Faced with the choice
   That it go or he go?

Alma Denny

Who's On First?

'You can be so inconsiderate.'

               'You are too sensitive.'

'Then why don't you take my feelings into consideration?'

                                        'If you

weren't so sensitive it wouldn't matter.'

           ·

'You seem to really care about me only when you want me to do
something for you.'

                  'You do too much for people.'

           ·

'I thought you were going home because you were too tired to go
with me to a bar.'

              'I was. But Norman didn't want to come here alone.'

           ·

'I'm awfully tired. Do you mind taking the subway home?'

                                       (Silence.)

'You could stay over . . .'

            (Silence.)

'I'll take you home.'

       (Silence.)

           ·

'Why do we have sex only when you want to?'

                                'Because you want

to have sex all the time.'

           ·

'Relationships work when two people equally desire to give to
each other.'

             'Relationships rarely work.'

'Do you love me?'

        'Of course –; but I resent it.'

.

'Why aren't you more affectionate?'

        'I am.'

.

'Couldn't we ever speak to each other without irony?'

        'Sure.'

.

'I love you, you know.'

        'Yes . . . but why?'

.

'Do you resent my advice?'

        'Yes. Especially because you're usually right.'

.

'Why do you like these paintings?'

        'What isn't there is more important than what is.'

.

'Your taste sometimes seems strange to me.'

        'I'm a Philistine.'

'A real Philistine would never admit it.'

        'I suppose you're right.'

.

'Aren't you interested in what I care about?'

        'Yes. But not now.'

.

'We should be more open with each other.'

        'Yes.'

'Shall we talk things over?'

        'What is there to say?'

'Are you ever going to cut down on your smoking?'

'It's all right
– I don't inhale.'

'Sometimes I get very annoyed with you.'

'The world is annoying.'

'Your cynicism is too easy.'

'Words interfere with the expression
of complex realities.'

'Do you enjoy suffering?'

'You can't work if you don't suffer.'
'But we suffer anyway.'

'I know.'

'Do you think we ever learn anything?'

'I've learned to do without.'

'You're always so negative.'

'I feel death all the time.'
'Are you afraid of anything?'

'Not working.'

'What shall we do for dinner?'

'It doesn't matter – whatever you'd like.'

'Why don't you care more?'

'I do.'

Lloyd Schwartz

IS THIS THE REAL THING?

If it is the real thing then these poems will make you feel even better and if it's not then you'll know what you are missing. One permanently lovelorn friend described 'Two Drops' as the poem that constantly reconfirms her faith in true love. I have included the Dorothy Parker poem by way of cautionary small print which you skip at your peril.

Giving Up Smoking

There's not a Shakespeare sonnet
Or a Beethoven quartet
That's easier to like than you
Or harder to forget.

You think that sounds extravagant?
I haven't finished yet –
I like you more than I would like
To have a cigarette.

Wendy Cope

Two Drops

No time to grieve for roses, when the forests are burning — SLOWACKI

The forests were on fire —
they however
wreathed their necks with their hands
like bouquets of roses

People ran to the shelters —
he said his wife had hair
in whose depths one could hide

Covered by one blanket
they whispered shameless words
the litany of those who love

When it got very bad
they leapt into each other's eyes
and shut them firmly

So firmly they did not feel the flames
when they came up to the eyelashes

To the end they were brave
To the end they were faithful
To the end they were similar
like two drops
stuck at the edge of a face

Zbigniew Herbert
translated from the Polish by Peter Dale Scott

Unfortunate Coincidence

By the time you swear you're his,
  Shivering and sighing,
And he vows his passion is
  Infinite, undying –
Lady, make a note of this:
  One of you is lying.

Dorothy Parker

What It Is

It is madness
says reason
It is what it is
says love

It is unhappiness
says caution
It is nothing but pain
says fear
It has no future
says insight
It is what it is
says love

It is ridiculous
says pride
It is foolish
says caution
It is impossible
says experience
It is what it is
says love

Eric Fried
translated from the German by Stuart Hood

The Clod and the Pebble

'Love seeketh not Itself to please,
'Nor for itself hath any care,
'But for another gives its ease,
'And builds a Heaven in Hell's despair.'

So sung a little Clod of Clay
Trodden with the cattle's feet,
But a Pebble of the brook
Warbled out these metres meet:

'Love seeketh only Self to please,
'To bind another to Its delight,
'Joys in another's loss of ease,
'And builds a Hell in Heaven's despite.'

William Blake
From *Songs of Experience*

JUST DO IT

Carpe diem, seize the day. These poems have everything you'll find in self-help books like 'Seven Habits of Highly Successful People', in a few lines. Take two minutes and get motivated. The MacNeice poem certainly worked for me. 'Tiger' is the poem to give your child when they hit adult life: 'to thine own self be true.'

And the days are not full enough

And the days are not full enough
And the nights are not full enough
And life slips by like a field mouse
                    Not shaking the grass.

Ezra Pound

Tiger

At noon the paper tigers roar – Miroslav Holub

The paper tigers roar at noon;
The sun is hot, the sun is high.
They roar in chorus, not in tune,
Their plaintive, savage hunting cry.

O, when you hear them, stop your ears
And clench your lids and bite your tongue.
The harmless paper tiger bears
Strong fascination for the young.

His forest is the busy street;
His dens the forum and the mart;
He drinks no blood, he tastes no meat:
He riddles and corrupts the heart.

But when the dusk begins to creep
From tree to tree, from door to door,
The jungle tiger wakes from sleep
And utters his authentic roar.

It bursts the night and shakes the stars
Till one breaks blazing from the sky;
Then listen! If to meet it soars
Your heart's reverberating cry,

My child, then put aside your fear:
Unbar the door and walk outside!
The real tiger waits you there;
His golden eyes shall be your guide.

And, should he spare you in his wrath,
The world and all the worlds are yours;
And should he leap the jungle path
And clasp you with his bloody jaws,

Then say, as his divine embrace
Destroys the mortal parts of you:
I too am of that royal race
Who do what we are born to do.

A. D. Hope

The slow starter

A watched clock never moves, they said:
Leave it alone and you'll grow up.
Nor will the sulking holiday train
Start sooner if you stamp your feet.
   He left the clock to go its way;
   The whistle blew, the train went gay.

Do not press me so, she said;
Leave me alone and I will write
But not just yet, I am sure you know
The problem. Do not count the days.
   He left the calendar alone;
   The postman knocked, no letter came.

O never force the pace, they said;
Leave it alone, you have lots of time,
Your kind of work is none the worse
For slow maturing. Do not rush.
   He took their tip, he took his time,
   And found his time and talent gone.

Oh you have had your chance, It said;
Left it alone and it was one.
Who said a watched clock never moves?
Look at it now. Your chance was I.
   He turned and saw the accusing clock
   Race like a torrent round a rock.

Louis MacNeice

MONDAY MORNING

There must be people who leap out of bed in the morning with a smile on their lips and a song in their heart, but I'm certainly not one of them. This poem by Romanian poet Nina Cassian tells it like it is. And if you need more reasons to get out of bed then turn to the poems in the 'Just Do It' section. Things will look better when you've had some coffee.

Morning Exercises

I wake up and say: I'm through.
It's my first thought at dawn.
What a nice way to start the day
with such a murderous thought.

God, take pity on me
— is the second thought, and then
I get out of bed
and live as if
nothing had been said.

Nina Cassian
translated from the Romanian
by Andrea Deletant and Brenda Walker

MONEY WORRIES

No poem will make that pile of bills any smaller but these might make it seem less daunting.

Fatigue

I'm tired of Love: I'm still more tired of Rhyme.
But Money gives me pleasure all the time.

Hilaire Belloc

Money

That money talks
I won't deny.
I heard it once.
It said, 'Goodbye.'

Richard Armour

MORNING AFTER

These poems are for those days when things seem to have shifted overnight. 'Apple Blossom' is a wonderful poem – the world can change, it all depends on how you look at it. Hugo Williams's poem is the perfect post-coital parlour game; and Dorothy Parker provides the small print as always.

Saturday Morning

Everyone who made love the night before
was walking around with flashing red lights
on top of their heads – a white-haired old gentleman,
a red-faced schoolboy, a pregnant woman
who smiled at me from across the street
and gave a little secret shrug,
as if the flashing red light on her head
was a small price to pay for what she knew.

Hugo Williams

The Flaw in Paganism

Drink and dance and laugh and lie,
  Love, the reeling midnight through,
For tomorrow we shall die!
  (But, alas, we never do.)

Dorothy Parker

Apple Blossom

The first blossom was the best blossom
For the child who never had seen an orchard;
For the youth whom whisky had led astray
The morning after was the first day.

The first apple was the best apple
For Adam before he heard the sentence;
When the flaming sword endorsed the Fall
The trees were his to plant for all.

The first ocean was the best ocean
For the child from streets of doubt and litter;
For the youth for whom the skies unfurled
His first love was his first world.

But the first verdict seemed the worst verdict
When Adam and Eve were expelled from Eden;
Yet when the bitter gates clanged to
The sky beyond was just as blue.

For the next ocean is the first ocean
And the last ocean is the first ocean
And, however, often the sun may rise,
A new thing dawns upon our eyes.

For the last blossom is the first blossom
And the first blossom is the best blossom
And when from Eden we take our way
The morning after is the first day.

Louis MacNeice

MOTHERS-IN-LAW

I hesitated about including this category, but this is such a good poem about a power struggle that so many of us are familiar with that I couldn't resist it. And if my own mother-in-law is reading this then I refer her to the apology section forthwith.

My Rival's House

is peopled with many surfaces.
Ormolu and gilt, slipper satin,
lush velvet couches,
cushions so stiff you can't sink in.
Tables polished clear enough to see the distortions in.

We take our shoes off at her door,
shuffle stocking-soled, tiptoe – the parquet floor
is beautiful and its surface must
be protected. Dust
cover, drawn shade,
won't let the surface colour fade.

Silver sugar-tongs and silver salver
my rival serves us tea.
She glosses over him and me.
I am all edges, a surface, a shell
And yet my rival thinks she means me well.
But what squirms beneath her surface I can tell.
Soon, my rival
capped tooth, polished nail

will fight, fight foul for her survival.
Deferential, daughterly, I sip
and thank her nicely for each bitter cup.

And I have much to thank her for.
This son she bore –
first blood to her –
never, never can escape scot free
the sour potluck of family.
And oh how close
this family that furnishes my rival's place.

Lady of the house.
Queen bee.
She is far more unconscious
far more dangerous than me.
Listen, I was always my own worst enemy.
She has taken even this from me.

She dishes up her dreams for breakfast.
Dinner, and her salt tears pepper our soup.
She won't
give up.

Liz Lochhead

MOVING HOUSE

In the top three of stressful rites of passage, moving house is a much more loaded decision than we generally admit. These poems are a timely reminder that you can move house but you can't leave your emotional baggage behind. The Ted Hughes poem, taken from his book *Birthday Letters* about his marriage to Sylvia Plath, is particularly acute about the fragility of fresh starts.

Cold Night

A long time in one place and I always think of moving;
then I run into the same trouble and I'm sorry I made the
  change.
I raise the wick of the cold lamp but the flame is out,
rake up what's left of the fire but it's turned to ashes.
Icy water drips a while and then stops;
windy blinds flap open and shut.
I know well enough what writing should avoid,
but thoughts come, and sorrow just somehow appears.

Ch'en Shih-Tao

translated from the Chinese by Burton Watson

When you are Moving into a New House

When you are moving into a new house
be slow to write the address in your address books,
because the ghosts who are named there
are constantly seeking new homes,
like fresher students in rain-steamed phone booths.

So by the time you arrive with your books
and frying pan, these ghosts are already
familiar with that easy chair, have found
slow, slow creaks in the floorboards,
are camped on the dream shores of that virgin bed.

Pat Boran

The Pan

When he stopped at last in the long main street
Of the small town, after that hundred
And ninety miles, the five-o'clock, September,
Brassy, low, wet Westcountry sun
Above the street's far end, and when
He had extricated his stiffness
From the car crammed with books, carrier bags
Of crockery, cutlery and baby things,
And crossed the tilting street in that strange town
To buy a pan to heat milk and babyfood
The moment they arrived
Hours ahead of their furniture
Into their stripped new house, in their strange new life,
He did not notice that the ironmonger's
Where he bought the pan had been closed
And empty for two years. And returning
With the little pan he did not notice
A man on the pavement staring at him,
His arm round a young woman who wore
A next-to-nothing long evening dress
Slashed to the hip, and a white, silk, open-work shawl
Round her naked shoulders, and leopard-claw ear-rings,
He did not recognize, nor did his wife
As he squeezed back weary beside her
Behind the wheel of the Morris Traveller,
That this man, barely two yards from them,
Staring at them both so fixedly,

The man so infinitely more alive
Than either of them there in the happy car
Was himself – knowing their whole future
And helpless to warn them.

Ted Hughes

NEW BABY

People tell you about the end of sleep when you have a new baby, but before the birth you can't imagine it and later you forget. I like the Thom Gunn poem because it makes sense of that inconsolable crying, and the other two poems express those two unwelcome emotions that face every new mother: fear and exasperation.

Lullaby

Go to sleep, Mum,
I won't stop breathing
suddenly, in the night.

Go to sleep, I won't
climb out of my cot and
tumble downstairs.

Mum, I won't swallow
the pills the doctor gave you or
put hairpins in electric
sockets, just go to sleep.

I won't cry
when you take me to school and leave me:
I'll be happy with other children
my own age.

Sleep, Mum, sleep.
I won't
fall in the pond, play with matches,
run under a lorry or even consider
sweets from strangers.

No, I won't
give you a lot of lip,
not like some.

I won't sniff glue,
fail all my exams,
get myself/
my girlfriend pregnant.
I'll work hard and get a steady/
really worthwhile job.
I promise, go to sleep.

I'll never forget
to drop in/phone/write
and if
I need any milk, I'll yell.

Rosemary Norman

Baby Song

From the private ease of Mother's womb
I fall into the lighted room.

Why don't they simply put me back
Where it is warm and wet and black?

But one thing follows on another.
Things were different inside Mother.

Padded and jolly I would ride
The perfect comfort of her inside.

They tuck me in a rustling bed
— I lie there, raging, small, and red.

Thom Gunn

If You'll Just Go To Sleep

The blood red rose
I gathered yesterday,
and the fire and cinnamon
of the carnation,

Bread baked with
anise seed and honey,
and a fish in a bowl
that makes a glow:

All this is yours,
baby born of woman,
if you'll *just*
go to sleep.

A rose, I say!
I say a carnation!
Fruit, I say!
And I say honey!

A fish that glitters!
And more, I say –
If you will *only*
sleep till day.

Gabriela Mistral
translated from the Spanish by Langston Hughes

The Child Is Like A Sailor Cast Up By The Sea

The child is like a sailor cast up by the sea,
Lying naked on the shore, unable to speak,
Helpless, when first it comes to the light of day,
Shed from the womb through all the pains of labour,
And fills the place with cries as well it might,
Having a life of so many ills before it.
Yet flocks and herds, to say nothing of wild beasts,
Don't need a rattle or anything of that kind
Nor even a nurse to feed them with baby talk:
Nor do they need sets of clothes for summer and winter.
One may add that they don't need weapons or high walls
To keep them safe, they find themselves perfectly happy
Walking around in a world which produces plenty.

from *De Rerum Natura*, Book 5
Lucretius
translated by C. H. Sisson

NEW YEAR'S RESOLUTIONS

A good poem to read over a cup of coffee and a cigarette, ten days after your New Year's resolution to give up smoking (although giving up smoking really will save your life).

The New Regime

Yes, I agree. We'll pull ourselves together.
We eat too much. We're always getting pissed.
It's not a bad idea to find out whether
We like each other sober. Let's resist.
I've got the Perrier and the carrot-grater,
I'll look on a Scotch or a pudding as a crime.
We all have to be sensible sooner or later
But don't let's be sensible all the time.

No more thinking about a second bottle
And saying 'What the hell?' and giving in.
Tomorrow I'll be jogging at full throttle
To make myself successful, rich and thin.
A healthy life's a great rejuvenator
But, God, it's going to be an uphill climb.
We all have to be sensible sooner or later
But don't let's be sensible all the time.

The conversation won't be half as trivial –
You'll hold forth on the issues of the day –
And, when our evenings aren't quite so convivial,
You'll start remembering the things I say.

Oh, see if you can catch the eye of the waiter
And order me a double vodka and lime.
We all have to be sensible sooner or later
But I refuse to be sensible all the time.

Wendy Cope

PARENTHOOD

If you read 'This Be The Verse' early enough, it could save you a fortune in therapy. The Ogden Nash couplet is for any parent with teenagers and the poem by the American poet Sharon Olds is the one to read when they finally leave home and the hole they leave is bigger than you thought possible.

The Parent

Children aren't happy with nothing to ignore,
And that's what parents were created for.

Ogden Nash

Forty-One, Alone, No Gerbil

In the strange quiet, I realise
there's no one else in the house. No bucktooth
mouth pulls at a stainless-steel teat, no
hairy mammal runs on a treadmill –
Charlie is dead, the last of our children's half-children.
When our daughter found him lying in the shavings, trans-
mogrified backwards from a living body
into a bolt of rodent bread
she turned her back on early motherhood
and went on single, with nothing. Crackers,
Fluffy, Pretzel, Biscuit, Charlie,
buried on the old farm we bought
where she could know nature. Well now she knows it
and it sucks. Creatures she loved, mobile and
needy, have gone down stiff and indifferent,
she will not adopt again though she cannot
have children yet, her body like a blueprint
of the understructure for a woman's body,
so now everything stops for a while,
now I must wait many years
to hear in this house again the faint
powerful call of a young animal.

Sharon Olds

This Be The Verse

They fuck you up, your mum and dad.
   They may not mean to, but they do.
They fill you with the faults they had
   And add some extra, just for you.

But they were fucked up in their turn
   By fools in old-style hats and coats,
Who half the time were soppy-stern
   And half at one another's throats.

Man hands on misery to man.
   It deepens like a coastal shelf.
Get out as early as you can,
   And don't have any kids yourself.

Philip Larkin

PLAYING AWAY

I was going to call this section 'infidelity', but in the interests of being discreet I've opted for the euphemism. If you've just started an affair the poems here may seem a bit bleak, so you might want to move quickly on to the 'Is It the Real Thing?' section, and who knows it may all work out. But if your particular double life has been up and running for a while then you'll recognize these poems as being spot on at describing that point where the impossible meets the irresistible.

Adultery

Wear dark glasses in the rain.
Regard what was unhurt
as though through a bruise.
Guilt. A sick, green tint.

New gloves, money tucked in the palms,
the handshake crackles. Hands
can do many things. Phone.
Open the wine. Wash themselves. Now

you are naked under your clothes all day,
slim with deceit. Only the once
brings you alone to your knees,
miming, more, more, older and sadder,

creative. Suck a lie with a hole in it
on the way home from a lethal, thrilling night
up against a wall, faster. Language
unpeels to a lost cry. You're a bastard.

Do it do it do it. Sweet darkness
in the afternoon; a voice in your ear
telling you how you are wanted,
which way, now. A telltale clock

wiping the hours from its face, your face
on a white sheet, gasping, radiant, yes.
Pay for it in cash, fiction, cab-fares back
to the life which crumbles like a wedding-cake.

Paranoia for lunch; too much
to drink, as a hand on your thigh
tilts the restaurant. You know all about love,
don't you. Turn on your beautiful eyes

for a stranger who's dynamite in bed, again
and again; a slow replay in the kitchen
where the slicing of innocent onions
scalds you to tears. Then, selfish autobiographical sleep

in a marital bed, the tarnished spoon of your body
stirring betrayal, your heart overripe at the core.
You're an expert, darling; your flowers
dumb and explicit on nobody's birthday.

So write the script – illness and debt,
a ring thrown away in the garden
no moon can heal, your own words
commuting to bile in your mouth, terror –

and all for the same thing twice. And all
for the same thing twice. You did it.
What. Didn't you. Fuck. Fuck. No. That was
the wrong verb. This is only an abstract noun.

Carol Ann Duffy

Prayer

God give me strength to lead a double life.
Cut me in half.
Make each half happy in its own way
with what is left. Let me disobey
my own best instincts
and do what I want to do, whatever that may be,
without regretting it, or thinking I might.

When I come home late at night from home,
saying I have to go away,
remind me to look out the window
to see which house I'm in.
Pin a smile on my face
when I turn up two weeks later with a tan
and presents for everyone.

Teach me how to stand and where to look
when I say the words
about where I've been
and what sort of time I've had.
Was it good or bad or somewhere in between?
I'd like to know how I feel about these things,
perhaps you'd let me know?

When it's time to go to bed in one of my lives,
go ahead of me up the stairs,
shine a light in the corners of my room.

Tell me this: do I wear pyjamas here,
or sleep with nothing on?
If you can't oblige by cutting me in half,
God give me strength to lead a double life.

Hugo Williams

Sigh no more Ladies

Sigh no more Ladies, sigh no more,
   Men were deceivers ever;
One foot in sea, and one on shore,
   To one thing constant never.
Then sigh not so, but let them go,
   And be you blithe and bonny,
Converting all your sounds of woe
   Into hey nonny nonny.

Sing no more ditties, sing no moe
   Of dumps so dull and heavy;
The fraud of men were ever so
   Since summer first was leavy.
Then sigh not so, but let them go,
   And be you blithe and bonny,
Converting all your sounds of woe
   Into hey nonny nonny.

William Shakespeare, *Much Ado About Nothing*

RETAIL THERAPY

Essential reading if you have a wallet full of storecards. It's not getting what you want, it's wanting what you get.

Shopper

I am spending my way out
of a recession. The road chokes
on delivery vans.

I used to be Just Looking Round,
I used to be How Much, and
Have You Got it in Beige.

Now I devour whole stores –
high speed spin; giant size; chunky gold;
de luxe springing. Things.

I drag them round me into a stockade.
It is dark inside; but my credit cards
are incandescent.

Connie Bensley

ROCK BOTTOM

If you've ever been clinically depressed, you'll know about what Emily Dickinson calls the 'hour of lead'. But if you've come through you'll know that in the end there is a letting go. If you are at rock bottom at the moment, take heart from these poems, the hour of lead will pass, there may even be a time when you remember it fondly. And if you are even thinking of harming yourself then read Dorothy Parker's 'Resume', to remind yourself of the practical difficulties.

I May Live On

I may live on until
I long for this time
In which I am so unhappy,
And remember it fondly.

Nagaraeba
Mata kono goro ya
Shinobaremu
Ushi to mishi yo zo
Ima wa koishiki

Fujiwara No Kiyosuke
translated from the Japanese by Kenneth Rexroth

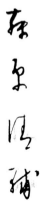

Not Waving But Drowning

Nobody heard him, the dead man,
But still he lay moaning:
I was much further out than you thought
And not waving but drowning.

Poor chap, he always loved larking
And now he's dead
It must have been too cold for him his heart gave way,
They said.

Oh, no no no, it was too cold always
(Still the dead one lay moaning)
I was much too far out all my life
And not waving but drowning.

Stevie Smith

After great pain, a formal feeling comes

After great pain, a formal feeling comes —
The Nerves sit ceremonious, like Tombs —
The stiff Heart questions was it He, that bore,
And Yesterday, or Centuries before?

The Feet, mechanical, go round —
Of Ground, or Air, or Ought —
A Wooden way
Regardless grown,
A Quartz contentment, like a stone —

This is the Hour of Lead —
Remembered, if outlived,
As Freezing persons, recollect the Snow —
First — Chill — then Stupor — then the letting go —

Emily Dickinson

Résumé

Razors pain you;
Rivers are damp;
Acids stain you;
And drugs cause cramp.
Guns aren't lawful;
Nooses give;
Gas smells awful;
You might as well live.

Dorothy Parker

S.A.D.

These days it is a syndrome called Seasonal Affective Disorder, but in the seventeenth century they suffered in 'the year's midnight' too. St Lucy's Day is the winter solstice, 21 December.

A Nocturnal upon St Lucy's Day, being the shortest day

'Tis the year's midnight, and it is the day's,
Lucy's, who scarce seven hours herself unmasks;
    The sun is spent, and now his flasks
    Send forth light squibs, no constant rays;
        The world's whole sap is sunk;
The general balm the hydroptic earth hath drunk,
Whither, as to the bed's-feet, life is shrunk,
Dead and interred; yet all these seem to laugh,
Compared with me, who am their epitaph.

Study me then, you who shall lovers be
At the next world, that is, at the next spring:
    For I am every dead thing,
    In whom love wrought new alchemy.
        For his art did express
A quintessence even from nothingness,
From dull privations, and lean emptinesss:
He ruined me, and I am re-begot
Of absence, darkness, death: things which are not.

All others, from all things, draw all that's good,
Life, soul, form, spirit, whence they being have;
   I, by Love's limbeck, am the grave
   Of all, that's nothing. Oft a flood
      Have we two wept, and so
Drowned the whole world, us two; oft did we grow
To be two Chaoses, when we did show
Care to ought else; and often absences
Withdrew our souls, and made us carcasses.

But I am by her death (which word wrongs her)
Of the first nothing the elixir grown;
   Were I a man, that I were one,
   I needs must know; I should prefer,
      If I were any beast,
Some ends, some means; yea plants, yea stones detest
And love; all, all some properties invest;
If I an ordinary nothing were,
As shadow, a light, and body must be here.

But I am None; nor will my sun renew.
You lovers, for whose sake the lesser sun
   At this time to the Goat is run
   To fetch new lust, and give it you,
      Enjoy your summer all;
Since she enjoys her long night's festival,
Let me prepare towards her, and let me call
This hour her vigil, and her eve, since this
Both the year's and the day's deep midnight is.

John Donne

114

SCHOOL

A poem for all over-anxious under-achievers: it all evens out in the end.

Streemin

Im in the botom streme
Which meens Im not brigth
dont like reading
cant hardly write

but all these divishns
arnt reely fair
look at the cemtery
no streemin there

Roger McGough

STAYING MARRIED

I included these poems on the basis that marriages can go up as well as down.
These poems are all testimonials to the pleasures of staying married. Even if you
are having problems it is worth reading these to remind yourself of the
consolations of the long haul, the long term dividends of leaving your love
invested in the same bond. I think Seamus Heaney's poem 'The Skunk' deserves a
special mention not only because it's a wonderful poem, but unusually in a poem
about marriage, it's also wonderfully erotic.

Valentine for a Middle-aged Spouse

Dear Love, since we might both be dead by now
through war, disease, hijack or accident
at least for one day let's not speak of how
much we have bickered, botched and badly spent.
Wouldn't it make much more sense to collude
in an affectionate work of camouflage,
turning our eyes away from all we've skewed,
to the small gains of household bricolage?
As our teeth loosen and our faces crag
(I shall grow skinnier as you grow paunched,
a Laurel to your Hardy, not much brag),
I'll think of all our love most sweetly launched
if you will look with favour on these lines
we may still live as tender valentines.

Elaine Feinstein

The Skunk

Up, black, striped and damasked like the chasuble
At a funeral mass, the skunk's tail
Paraded the skunk. Night after night
I expected her like a visitor.

The refrigerator whinnied into silence.
My desk light softened beyond the veranda.
Small oranges loomed in the orange tree.
I began to be tense as a voyeur.

After eleven years I was composing
Love-letters again, broaching the word 'wife'
Like a stored cask, as if its slender vowel
Had mutated into the night earth and air

Of California. The beautiful, useless
Tang of eucalyptus spelt your absence.
The aftermath of a mouthful of wine
Was like inhaling you off a cold pillow.

And there she was, the intent and glamorous,
Ordinary, mysterious skunk,
Mythologized, demythologized,
Snuffing the boards five feet beyond me.

It all came back to me last night, stirred
By the sootfall of your things at bedtime,
Your head-down, tall-up hunt in a bottom drawer
For the black plunge-line nightdress.

Dear Diary

Today my wife called me
    a 'pompous old fart'.
We were hugging at the time
    and did not spring apart,
though her words were deliberate
    and struck at my heart.

It's a fearsome business,
    this loving and being loved.
Would anyone try it
    if they hadn't been shoved
by a force beyond resistance –
    velvet-fisted and iron-gloved?

Christopher Reid

STRESSED OUT

The notion that time is the biggest luxury of all has become a cliché, but the millions of people who bought *The Little Book of Calm* instead of sitting down and putting their feet up attest to its veracity. Before you return those calls, read these poems and spend a good long time looking out of the window.

Miscellaneous Poem

Clouds appear free of care
And carefree drift away.
But the carefree mind is not to be 'found' –
To find it, first stop looking around.

Wang An Shih

When You've Got

When you've got the plan of your life
matched to the time it will take
but you just want to press SHIFT/BREAK
and print over and over
this is not what I was after
this is not what I was after.

when you've finally stripped out the house
with its iron-cold fireplace,
its mouldings, its mortgage,
its single-skin walls
but you want to write in the plaster
'This is not what I was after.'

when you've got the rainbow-clad baby
in his state-of-the-art pushchair
but he arches his back at you
and pulps his Activity Centre
and you just want to whisper
'This is not what I was after.'

when the vacuum seethes and whines in the lounge
and the waste-disposal unit blows,
when tenners settle in your account
like snow hitting a stove,
when you get a chat from your spouse
about marriage and personal growth,

when a wino comes to sleep in your porch
on your Citizen's Charter
and you know a hostel's opening soon
but your headache's closer
and you really just want to torch
the bundle of rags and newspaper

and you'll say to the newspaper
'This is not what we were after,
this is not what we were after.'

Helen Dunmore

Reflexions

Let me do my work each day;
and if the darkened hours
of despair overcome me, may I
not forget the strength
that comforted me in the
desolation of other times. May I
still remember the bright
hours that found me walking
over the silent hills of my
childhood, or dreaming on the
margin of the quiet river,
when a light glowed within me,
and I promised my early God
to have courage amid the
tempests of the changing years.
Spare me from bitterness
and from the sharp passions of
unguarded moments. May
I not forget that poverty and
riches are of the spirit.
Though the world know me not,
may my thoughts and actions
be such as shall keep me friendly
with myself. Lift my eyes
from the earth, and let me not
forget the uses of the stars.
Forbid that I should judge others
lest I condemn myself.

Let me not follow the clamour of
the world, but walk calmly
in my path. Give me a few friends
who will love me for what
I am; and keep ever burning
before my vagrant steps
the kindly light of hope. And
though age and infirmity overtake
me, and I come not within
sight of the castle of my dreams,
teach me still to be thankful
for life, and for time's olden
memories that are good and
sweet; and may the evening's
twilight find me gentle still.

Max Ehrmann

SUCCESSFULLY SINGLE

If you're newly single then you may not be ready for these poems and might find more solace in the 'When Your Lover Has Gone' section. But if you have got to the stage when you feel that you really are better off without him or her, then read on. And if you've always been successfully single you will be hugely relieved to find some poems that don't turn you into Eleanor Rigby or even Bridget Jones.

eating alone
my alphabet soup
speaks to me

Brenda S. Duster

Against Coupling

I write in praise of the solitary act:
of not feeling a trespassing tongue
forced into one's mouth, one's breath
smothered, nipples crushed against the
ribcage, and that metallic tingling
in the chin set off by a certain odd nerve:

unpleasure. Just to avoid those eyes would help –
such eyes as a young girl draws life from,
listening to the vegetal
rustle within her, as his gaze
stirs polypal fronds in the obscure
sea-bed of her body, and her own eyes blur.

There is much to be said for abandoning
this no longer novel exercise –
for not 'participating in
a total experience' – when
one feels like the lady in Leeds who
had seen *The Sound of Music* eighty-six times;

or more, perhaps, like the school drama mistress
producing *A Midsummer Night's Dream*
for the seventh year running, with
yet another cast from 5 B.
Pyramus and Thisbe are dead, but
the hole in the wall can still be troublesome.

I advise you, then, to embrace it without
encumbrance. No need to set the scene,
dress up (or undress), make speeches.
Five minutes of solitude are
enough – in the bath, or to fill
that gap between the Sunday papers and lunch.

Fleur Adcock

Love After Love

The time will come
when, with elation,
you will greet yourself arriving
at your own door, in your own mirror,
and each will smile at the other's welcome,

and say, sit here. Eat.
You will love again the stranger who was your self.
Give wine. Give bread. Give back your heart
to itself, to the stranger who has loved you

all your life, whom you ignored
for another, who knows you by heart.
Take down the love letters from the bookshelf,

the photographs, the desperate notes,
peel your own image from the mirror.
Sit. Feast on your life.

Derek Walcott

Go To Bed With A Cheese & Pickle Sandwich

Go to bed with a cheese and pickle sandwich
— it is life enhancing.
It doesn't chat you up
— *you* have to make *it*.

A cheese and pickle sandwich
is never disappointing.
You don't lie there thinking:
Am I too fat?
Too insecure?
Too fertile?

Your thoughts are clear
— your choices simple:
to cut it in half,
or not to cut it in half.
How thin to slice the cheese,
and where you should place the pickle.

From a cheese and pickle sandwich
you do not expect flowers,
poems, words of love and acts of adoration.
You expect what you get
— cheese . . . and pickle.

You want, you eat,
and afterwards – you have eaten.
No lying awake resentful
listening to it snore.

Safe snacks.
It comes
recommended.

Mandy Coe

WHEN YOU LOSE YOUR PET

Bereavement sounds tragic, pet bereavement sounds slightly absurd. And yet the death of a pet can be shattering and the lack of a conventional mould to pour that grief into can make it even worse. Perhaps these two poems can help you give the sadness a shape.

Praise of a Collie

She was a small dog, neat and fluid –
Even her conversation was tiny:
She greeted with you *bow*, never *bow-wow*.

Her sons stood monumentally over her
But did what she told them. Each grew grizzled
Till it seemed he was his own mother's grandfather.

Once, gathering sheep on a showery day,
I remarked how dry she was. Pollochan said, 'Ah,
It would take a very accurate drop to hit Lassie.'

She sailed in the dinghy like a proper sea-dog.
Where's a burn? – she's first on the other side.
She flowed through fences like a piece of black wind.

But suddenly she was old and sick and crippled . . .
I grieved for Pollochan when he took her a stroll
And put his gun to the back of her head.

Norman MacCaig

I had a dove and the sweet dove died

I had a dove and the sweet dove died;
   And I have thought it died of grieving:
Oh, what could it grieve for? Its feet were tied,
   With a silken thread of my own hand's weaving;
Sweet little red feet! why should you die –
Why should you leave me, sweet dove! why?
You liv'd alone on the forest-tree,
Why, pretty thing! could you not live with me?
I kiss'd you oft and gave you white peas;
Why not live sweetly, as in the green trees?

John Keats

WHEN YOUR LOVER HAS GONE

If it's just happened then read 'Advice to a Discarded Lover' immediately. It isn't comfortable reading but will help you avoid behaviour that will make you cringe when you remember it in the years to come. Instead of sobbing into an answering machine read Vasko Popa's scorching hate poem and put a hex on the faithless one instead. When the hurt has faded a little read 'Out of Danger' by James Fenton and 'The Art of Losing' by Elizabeth Bishop to reinforce your new found stoicism. But just when you think you have it all neatly stowed away, something you didn't plan for will bring all those memories swirling back and that's when you should read 'The *Darling* Letters' by Carol Ann Duffy.

Advice to a Discarded Lover

Think, now: if you have found a dead bird,
Not only dead, not only fallen,
But full of maggots: what do you feel –
More pity or more revulsion?

Pity is for the moment of death,
And the moments after. It changes
When decay comes, with the creeping stench
And the wriggling, munching scavengers.

Returning later, though, you will see
A shape of clean bone, a few feathers,
An inoffensive symbol of what
Once lived. Nothing to make you shudder.

It is clear then. But perhaps you find
The analogy I have chosen
For our dead affair rather gruesome –
Too unpleasant a comparison.

It is not accidental. In you
I see maggots close to the surface.
You are eaten up by self-pity,
Crawling with unlovable pathos.

If I were to touch you I should feel
Against my fingers fat, moist worm-skin.
Do not ask me for charity now:
Go away until your bones are clean.

Fleur Adcock

Loss

The day he moved out was terrible –
That evening she went through hell.
His absence wasn't a problem
But the corkscrew had gone as well.

Wendy Cope

Give Me Back My Rags

Just come to my mind
My thoughts will scratch out your face

Just come into my sight
My eyes will start snarling at you

Just open your mouth
My silence will smash your jaws

Just remind me of you
My remembering will paw up the ground under your feet

That's what it's come to between us.

Vasco Popa

Out of Danger

Heart be kind and sign the release
As the trees their loss approve.
Learn as leaves must learn to fall
Out of danger, out of love.

What belongs to frost and thaw
Sullen winter will not harm.
What belongs to wind and rain
Is out of danger from the storm.

Jealous passion, cruel need
Betray the heart they feed upon.
But what belongs to earth and death
Is out of danger from the sun.

I was cruel, I was wrong –
Hard to say and hard to know.
You do not belong to me.
You are out of danger now –

Out of danger from the wind,
Out of danger from the wave,
Out of danger from the heart
Falling, falling out of love.

James Fenton

One Art

The art of losing isn't hard to master;
so many things seem filled with the intent
to be lost that their loss is no disaster.

Lose something every day. Accept the fluster
of lost door keys, the hour badly spent.
The art of losing isn't hard to master.

Then practice losing farther, losing faster:
places, and names, and where it was you meant
to travel. None of these will bring disaster.

I lost my mother's watch. And look! my last, or
next-to-last, of three loved houses went.
The art of losing isn't hard to master.

I lost two cities, lovely ones. And, vaster,
some realms I owned, two rivers, a continent.
I miss them, but it wasn't a disaster.

– Even losing you (the joking voice, a gesture
I love) I shan't have lied. It's evident
the art of losing's not too hard to master
though it may look like (*Write* it!) like disaster.

Elizabeth Bishop

The *Darling* Letters

Some keep them in shoeboxes away from the light,
sore memories blinking out as the lid lifts,
their own recklessness written all over them. *My own . . .*
Private jokes, no longer comprehended, pull their punchlines,
fall flat in the gaps between endearments. *What
are you wearing?*

        Don't ever change.
They start with *Darling*; end in recriminations,
absence, sense of loss. Even now, the fist's bud flowers
into trembling, the fingers trace each line and see
the future then. *Always . . .* Nobody burns them,
the *Darling* letters, stiff in their cardboard coffins.

Babykins . . . We all had strange names
which make us blush, as though we'd murdered
someone under an alias, long ago. *I'll die
without you. Die.* Once in a while, alone,
we take them out to read again, the heart thudding
like a spade on buried bones.

Carol Ann Duffy

ACKNOWLEDGEMENTS

We are grateful for permission to reprint the following copyright poems in this collection:
FLEUR ADCOCK: 'Things', 'Against Coupling', and 'Advice to a Discarded Lover' from *Selected Poems* (OUP, 1983), © Fleur Adcock 1983, and 'Kissing' from *The Incident Book* (OUP, 1986), © Fleur Adcock 1986, both reprinted by permission of Oxford University Press. **MAYA ANGELOU:** 'Still I Rise' from *And Still I Rise* (Virago Press) reprinted by permission of Little Brown. **WANG AN-SHIH:** 'Miscellaneous Poem' trans. by Jan W Walls from *A Drifting Boat: Chinese Zen Poetry* ed. by J P Seaton and Dennis Maloney (White Pine Press, 1994). **W H AUDEN:** 'Twelve Songs IX' ('Funeral Blues'), from *Collected Poems*, reprinted by permission of the publisher, Faber & Faber Ltd. **HILAIRE BELLOC:** 'Fatigue' from *Complete Verse* (Duckworth, 1970), reprinted by permission of The Peters Fraser and Dunlop Group Ltd. on behalf of the Estate of Hilaire Belloc. **CONNIE BENSLEY:** 'God's Christmas Jokes' from *Central Reservations: New and Selected Poems* (Bloodaxe Books, 1990) and 'Shopper' from *Choosing to Be a Swan* (Bloodaxe Books, 1994), both reprinted by permission of the publisher. **ELIZABETH BISHOP:** 'One Art' from *The Complete Poems 1927–1979*, 1979, 1983 by Alice Helen Methfessel, reprinted by permission of Farrar, Straus & Giroux, LLC. **PAT BORAN:** 'When You Are Moving Into a New House', reprinted by permission of The Dedalus Press, Dublin. **NINA CASSIAN:** 'Morning Exercises', trans. by Brenda Walker and Andrea Deletant, from Nina Cassian: *Life Sentence* ed. by William Jay Smith (Anvil, 1990), reprinted by permission of Anvil Press Poetry Ltd. **RAYMOND CARVER:** 'Late Fragment' from *All Of Us: The Collected Poems* (first published in Great Britain 1996 by Harvill), © Tess Gallagher 1996, reprinted by permission of The Harvill Press. **C P CAVAFY:** 'Che fece ... il Gran Rifiuto' and 'As Much As You Can' from *Collected Poems* trans. by Edmund Keeley and Philip Sherrard (Hogarth Press, 1990) reprinted by permission of Random House Group on behalf of the Estate of C P Cavafy and the translators. **MANDY COE:** 'Go to Bed with a Cheese & Pickle Sandwich' first published in *Eating Your Cake and Having It* ed. by Ann Gray (Fatchance Press, 1997), reprinted by permission of the author. **WENDY COPE:** 'Bloody Men', 'The New Regime' and 'Loss' from *Serious Concerns* and 'Giving Up Smoking' from *Making Cocoa for Kingsley Amis*, all reprinted by permission of the publisher, Faber & Faber Ltd; 'How to Deal with the Press' and 'The Ted Williams Villanelle', both uncollected poems, reprinted by permission of the author. **W H DAVIES:** 'Leisure' from *Complete Poems* (Jonathan Cape) reprinted by permission of Dee & Griffin, Trustees of Mrs H M Davies Will Trust. **EMILY DICKINSON:** poem 341 ('After great pain, a formal feeling comes') from *Further Poems of Emily Dickinson* (Little Brown, 1929) reprinted by permission of Little Brown & Co. **HELEN DUNMORE:** 'When You've Got' from *Recovering a Body* (Bloodaxe Books, 1994), reprinted by permission of the publisher. **CAROL ANN DUFFY:** 'The *Darling* Letters' from *The Other Country* (Anvil, 1990) and 'Adultery' from *Mean Time* (Anvil, 1993), reprinted by permission of Anvil Press Poetry Ltd. **BRENDA DUSTER:**

Faber & Faber Ltd. **DENISE LEVERTOV:** 'Wedding-Ring' from *Selected Poems* (Bloodaxe Books, 1986), reprinted by permission of Laurence Pollinger Ltd on behalf of the author and the proprietors, New Directions Publishing Corporation. **LIZ LOCHHEAD:** 'My Rival's House' from *Dreaming Frankenstein and Other Poems* (Polygon, 1984), reprinted by permission of Edinburgh University Press Ltd. **LUCRETIUS:** 'The Child is Like a Sailor Cast Up by the Sea' from *De Rerum Natura*, Book 5, trans. by C H Sisson in *Collected Translations* (Carcanet, 1996), reprinted by permission of Carcanet Press Ltd. **NORMAN MACCAIG:** 'Praise of a Collie' from Collected Poems (Hogarth Press, 1990) reprinted by permission of Random House Group on behalf of the author. **ROGER MCGOUGH:** 'My Bus Conductor' from *The Mersey Sound* and 'Streemin' from *In The Glassroom* (Cape, 1976), reprinted by permission of The Peters Fraser and Dunlop Group Limited on behalf of Roger McGough. **LOUIS MACNEICE:** "The Slow Starter' and 'Apple Blossom' from *Collected Poems* (Faber), reprinted by permission of David Higham Associates. **GLYN MAXWELL:** 'The Perfect Match' from *Out of the Rain* (Bloodaxe Books, 1992), © Glyn Maxwell 1992, and 'Deep Sorriness Atonement Song' from *The Breakage* (Faber, 1998), © Glyn Maxwell 1998, reprinted by permission of Gillon Aitken Associates Ltd. **GABRIELA MISTRAL:** 'If You'll Just Go to Sleep' from *Selected Poems of Gabriela Mistral* trans. by Langston Hughes (Indiana University Press), © 1957 by the Estate of Gabriela Mistral and Langston Hughes, reprinted by permission of David Higham Associates. **EDWIN MUIR:** 'The Confirmation' from *Collected Poems*, reprinted by permission of the publisher, Faber & Faber Ltd. **OGDEN NASH:** 'The Parent' and Family Court' from *Candy Is Dandy: The Best of Ogden Nash* (Andre Deutsch), reprinted by permission of the publisher. **DOROTHY NIMMO:** 'A Woman's Work' from *Homewards* (Giant Steps, 1987), reprinted by permission of the author. **ROSEMARY NORMAN:** 'Lullaby' first published in *In the Gold of the Flesh* ed. by Rosemary Palmeira (Women's Press, 1990), © Rosemary Norman 1990, reprinted by permission of the author. **JULIE O'CALLAGHAN:** 'Managing the Common Herd: two approaches for management' from *What's What* (Bloodaxe Books, 1991), reprinted by permission of the publisher. **SHARON OLDS:** 'Forty-One, Alone, No Gerbil' from *The Wellspring* (Jonathan Cape, 1996), reprinted by permission of Random House Group on behalf of the author. **DOROTHY PARKER:** 'Social Note', 'Unfortunate Coincidence', 'The Flaw in Paganism' and 'Resumé' from *The Collected Dorothy Parker*, reprinted by permission of the publisher, Gerald Duckworth and Company Ltd. **VASKO POPA:** 'Give Me Back My Rags' trans. by Anne Pennington from *Vasko Popa: Collected Poems* trans. by Anne Pennington, revised and expanded by Francis R Jones (Anvil Press Poetry 1997), reprinted by permission of the publisher. **EZRA POUND:** 'And the days are not full enough' from *Collected Shorter Poems*, reprinted by permission of the publisher, Faber & Faber Ltd. **KURODO SABURO:** 'I am Completely Different' trans. by James Kirkup from James Kirkup: *Burning Giraffes: Modern and Contemporary Japanese Poetry* (University of Salzburg Press, 1996), reprinted by permission of James Kirkup. **LLOYD SCHWARZ:** 'Who's On First?' from *These People* (Wesleyan University Press, 1981) © 1981 by Lloyd Schwarz, reprinted by permission of The University Press of New England. **C H SISSON:** 'The Child is Like a Sailor Cast Up by the Sea' from *Collected Translations* (Carcanet, 1996) trans. from Lucretius: *De Rerum Natura*, Book 5, reprinted by permission of Carcanet Press Ltd. **STEVIE SMITH:** 'Not Waving but Drowning' from *The Collected Poems of Stevie Smith* (Penguin), reprinted by permission of James MacGibbon. **CH'EN SHIH-TAO:**

'Cold Night' trans. by Jonathan Chaves from *The Columbia Book of Later Chinese Poetry* ed. and trans. by Jonathan Chaves, © 1986 by Columbia University Press, reprinted by permission of the publisher. **TOM VAUGHAN**: 'Proposal', first published in *Orbis* 108/ 9, Spring/Summer 1998, reprinted by permission of the author. **DEREK WALCOTT:** 'Love After Love' from *Sea Grapes* (Jonathan Cape, 1976) reprinted by permission of Random House Group on behalf of the author. **ALICE WALKER:** 'I'm Really Very Fond' from *Horses Make a Landscape Look More Beautiful* (The Women's Press, 1985), reprinted by permission of David Higham Associates. **HUGO WILLIAMS:** 'Saturday Morning' and 'Prayer', reprinted by permission of the publisher, Faber & Faber Ltd. **W B YEATS:** 'The Collarbone of a Hare' and 'To a friend whose work has come to nothing' from *The Collected Works of W B Yeats Vol I: The Poems*, revised and edited by Richard J Finneran, © 1983, 1989 by Anne Yeats, by permission of A P Watt Ltd on behalf of Michael B Yeats.

Although we have tried to trace and contact all copyright holders before publication, this has not been possible in every case. If notified the publisher will be pleased to make any necessary arrangements at the earliest opportunity.

EMOTIONAL INDEX

apologies
Deep Sorriness Atonement
  Song GLYN
  MAXWELL 3

bad hair day
Still to be Neat
  BEN JONSON 5
The Fat Lady's Request
  JOYCE LA VERNE 6

bereavement
Do Not Stand At My Grave
  and Weep 7
Funeral Blues
  W H AUDEN 8
A Short Film
  TED HUGHES 9

big decision
Bloody Men
  WENDY COPE 10
Che Fece . . . Il Gran
  Rifiuto C P CAVAFY 11
The Road Not Taken
  ROBERT FROST 12

birthday blues
Stella's Birthday
  JONATHAN SWIFT 13
What Fifty Said
  ROBERT FROST 14

career crisis
Managing the Common
  Herd: two approaches for
  senior management
  JULIE
  O'CALLAGHAN 15
Toads PHILIP LARKIN 17

christmas
Family Court
  OGDEN NASH 19
God's Christmas Jokes
  CONNIE BENSLEY 20
Monstrous Ingratitude
  BORIS PARKIN 21

commitment problems
I'm Really Very Fond
  ALICE WALKER 22
The Collarbone of a Hare
  W B YEATS 24
Eternity WILLIAM
  BLAKE 25
Perpetual Motion TONY
  HOAGLAND 26

divorce
The Way We Live
  VICKI FEAVER 28
Wedding-Ring DENISE
  LEVERTOV 30
A Woman's Work
  DOROTHY NIMMO 31
The End of Love
  SOPHIE HANNAH 32

**don't let the bastards get
  you down**
If People Disapprove of
  You SOPHIE
  HANNAH 33
To a Friend Whose Work
  Has Come to Nothing
  W B YEATS 35
Invictus W E HENLEY 36
Still I Rise MAYA
  ANGELOU 37

famous for fifteen minutes
How to Deal with the Press
  WENDY COPE 39

first date
Proposal TOM
  VAUGHAN 41
Social Note DOROTHY
  PARKER 43

first wrinkle
Kissing
  FLEUR ADCOCK 44
Warning
  JENNY JOSEPH 45

football widow
The Perfect Match
  GLYN MAXWELL 46

friendship
extract from 'A Poison
  Tree' WILLIAM
  BLAKE 47

extract from sermon
JOHN DONNE 48
Friendship ELIZABETH
JENNINGS 49

getting married
extract from 'The Prophet'
KAHLIL GIBRAN 50
The Confirmation
EDWIN MUIR 51

hangover
Hock and Soda Water
GEORGE GORDON,
LORD BYRON 52

illness
My Busconductor ROGER
MCGOUGH 53
When I have Fears that I
may Cease to be
JOHN KEATS 55

insomnia
Things FLEUR
ADCOCK 56

instant moral fibre
If RUDYARD KIPLING 57
As Much as You Can
C P CAVAFY 59
extract from 'Poems
for Pirayé (His Wife)
From Prison'
NASIM HIKMET 60
Leisure W H DAVIES 61
I am Completely Different
KURODA SABURO 62
The Ted Williams Villanelle
(for Ari Badaines)
WENDY COPE 63

Late Fragment RAYMOND
CARVER 64

**is this relationship going
anywhere?**
Modern Love, Sonnet 17
GEORGE MEREDITH 65
Mrs Hobson's Choice
ALMA DENNY 66
Who's On First LLOYD
SCHWARTZ 67

is this the real thing?
Giving up Smoking
WENDY COPE 70
Two Drops ZBIGNIEW
HERBERT 71
Unfortunate Coincidence
DOROTHY PARKER 72
What It Is
ERICH FRIED 73
The Clod and the Pebble
WILLIAM BLAKE 74

just do it
And the days are not full
enough
EZRA POUND 75
Tiger A D HOPE 76
The slow starter LOUIS
MACNEICE 78

monday morning
Morning Exercises
NINA CASSIAN 79

money worries
Fatigue HILAIRE
BELLOC 80
Money RICHARD
ARMOUR 81

morning after
Saturday Morning
HUGO WILLIAMS 82
The Flaw in Paganism
DOROTHY PARKER 83
Apple Blossom
LOUIS MACNEICE 84

mothers-in-law
My Rival's House
LIZ LOCHHEAD 86

moving house
Cold Night
CH'EN SHIH-TAO 88
When You Are Moving Into
a New House
PAT BORAN 89
The Pan TED HUGHES 90

new baby
Lullaby
ROSEMARY
NORMAN 92
Baby Song
THOM GUNN 94
If You'll Just Go To Sleep
GABRIELA MISTRAL 95
The Child Is Like A Sailor …
LUCRETIUS 96

new year's resolutions
The New Regime
WENDY COPE 97

parenthood
The Parent
OGDEN NASH 99
Forty-one, Alone,
No Gerbil
SHARON OLDS 100

144

This Be The Verse
  PHILIP LARKIN 101

playing away
Adultery CAROL ANN
  DUFFY 102
Prayer HUGO
  WILLIAMS 105
Sigh no more Ladies,
  sigh no more . . .
  WILLIAM
  SHAKESPEARE 107

retail therapy
Shopper CONNIE
  BENSLEY 108

rock bottom
I May Live On
  FUJIWARA NO
  KIYOSUKE 109
Not Waving But
  Drowning
  STEVIE SMITH 110
After great pain, a
  formal feeling comes
  EMILY DICKINSON 111
Résumé DOROTHY
  PARKER 112

s.a.d.
A Nocturnal upon St Lucy's
  Day, being the shortest
  day JOHN DONNE 113

school
Streemin ROGER
  McGOUGH 115

staying married
Valentine for a Middle-Aged
  Spouse ELAINE
  FEINSTEIN 116
The Skunk SEAMUS
  HEANEY 117
Dear Diary CHRISTOPHER
  REID 118

stressed out
Miscellaneous Poem
  WANG AN SHIH 119
When You've Got
  HELEN DUNMORE 120
Reflexions
  MAX EHRMANN 122

successfully single
Eating Alone BRENDA
  S DUSTER 124

Against Coupling FLEUR
  ADCOCK 125
Love After Love DEREK
  WALCOTT 127
Go to Bed with a Cheese &
  Pickle Sandwich
  MANDY COE 128

when you lose your pet
Praise of a Collie NORMAN
  MACCAIG 130
I had a dove and the sweet
  dove died
  JOHN KEATS 131

when your lover has gone
Advice to a Discarded
  Lover FLEUR
  ADCOCK 132
Loss WENDY COPE 134
Give me Back My Rags
  VASCO POPA 135
Out of Danger
  JAMES FENTON 136
One Art ELIZABETH
  BISHOP 137
The *Darling* Letters CAROL
  ANN DUFFY 138

0 00 710650 5

Also by Daisy Goodwin:

101 POEMS
TO GET YOU THROUGH THE DAY (AND NIGHT)

A SURVIVAL KIT FOR MODERN LIFE